SUMMERTIME SLEEPERS

SUMMERTIME SLEEPERS

Animals That ~~HIBERNATE~~ ESTIVATE

Melissa Stewart

Illustrated by
Sarah S. Brannen

Charlesbridge

YAWN, STRETCH, BLINK!

As warm weather spreads across the land, hibernating animals spring to life.

But soon another group of animals searches for shelter. They settle into cool, snug spots and sink into a summertime sleep called *estivation*.

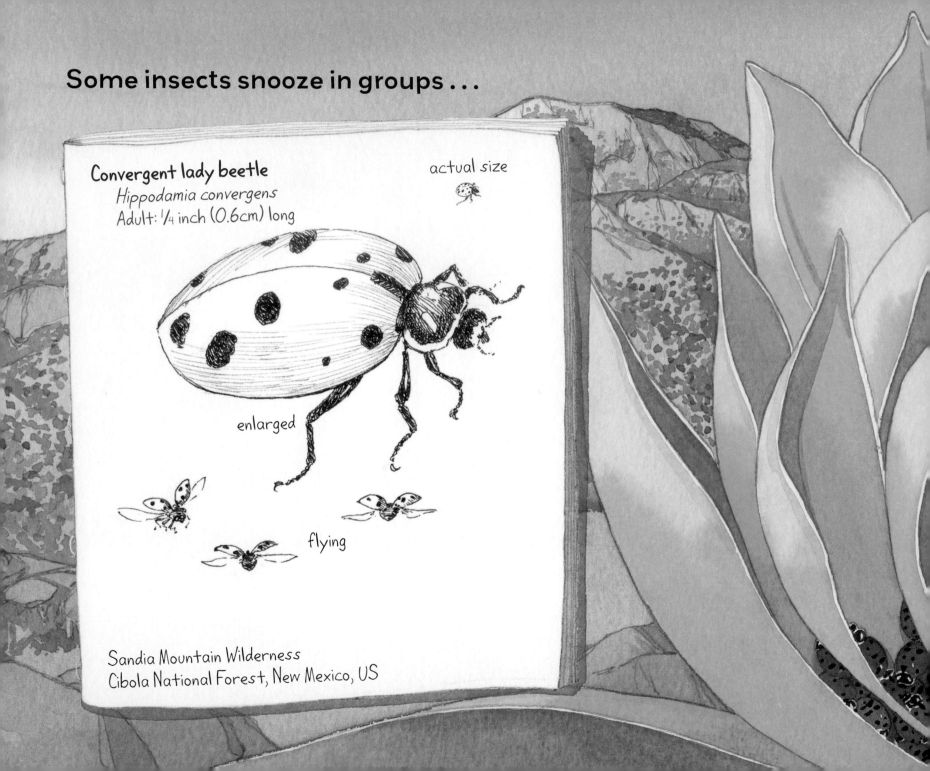

Convergent lady beetle
Hippodamia convergens
Adult: ¼ inch (0.6cm) long

actual size

enlarged

flying

Sandia Mountain Wilderness
Cibola National Forest, New Mexico, US

In hot, dry places, hundreds of ladybugs pile inside a curled-up cluster of leaves. Their hidden home keeps them safe while they sleep through summer.

. . . but others rest all alone.

Mourning cloak butterfly
Nymphalis antiopa
Adult: 3 inches (8 cm) wide

actual size

resting on oak leaf

Broughton Nature Area
Marietta, Ohio, US

A mourning cloak butterfly breaks out of its chrysalis in early summer. After guzzling tree sap for a few days, it slips into a crevice and nods off until the scent of fallen leaves fills the air.

Some hard-shelled creatures climb up high for a nap . . .

When the days grow long and hot, land snails cling to tree branches and seal their shells shut. Their heart rates slow, and they barely breathe as they wait for cooler days.

Land snail
Helix pomatia
Adult: 1½ inches (4 cm) wide

actual size

drinking a
drop of dew

Hunte River, Lower Saxony, Germany

Christmas Island red crab
  Gecarcoidea natalis
  Adult: 4 ½ inches (11 cm) wide

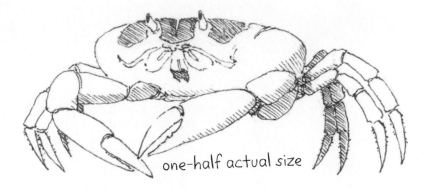

one-half actual size

migrating to ocean
to mate and lay eggs

Christmas Island National Park
Christmas Island, Australia

As the summer sun beats down, Christmas Island red crabs take refuge at the bottom of their burrows. Deep below the forest floor, they hunker down and sack out.

Some fish cozy up quickly . . .

For part of the year an African lungfish slithers and glides in a shallow, swampy pool. But when the water dries up, the fish burrows into the cool mud left behind. Slippery slime oozes out of its body, keeping the fish moist while it rests.

As the days heat up, a California tiger salamander scouts out an empty rodent hole and falls asleep. The cool, comfy burrow is the perfect place to spend summer.

. . . while others drift off in a nest
they've built themselves.

During the heat of summer, a pixie frog digs a
hole in the ground, wraps itself inside a cocoon,
and takes a good long break. When the rainy
season returns, the frog rips off its wrapper,
eats it, and then scrambles to the surface.

Pixie frog
Pyxicephalus adspersus
Adult: 4 to 8 inches (10 to 20 cm) long

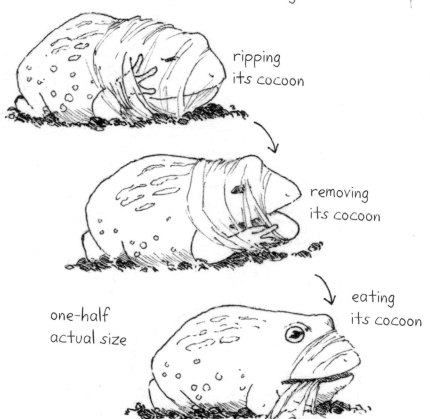

ripping
its cocoon

removing
its cocoon

eating
its cocoon

one-half
actual size

Central Kalahari Game Reserve, Botswana

Some reptiles go on long journeys
before they relax and repose . . .

Spotted turtle
Clemmys guttata
Adult: 3 ½ to 4 ½ inches (9 to 11 cm) long

actual size

digging

Oak Knoll Wildlife Sanctuary
Attleboro, Massachusetts, US

In spring, a spotted turtle travels to a vernal pool to gorge on amphibian eggs and tadpoles. But when the part-time pool dries up, the turtle has trouble finding food. It migrates to higher ground, burrows into forest leaf litter, and conks out all summer long.

... but others stay at home to snooze.

Common leopard gecko
Eublepharis macularius
Adult: 7 ½ to 11 inches (19 to 28 cm) long

actual size

Karoonjhar Mountains, Pakistan

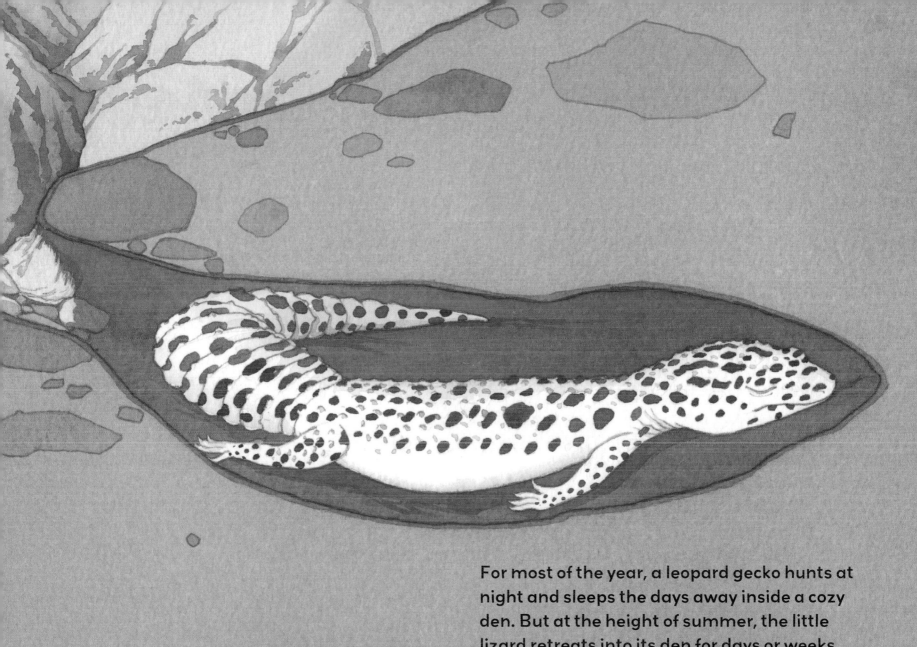

For most of the year, a leopard gecko hunts at night and sleeps the days away inside a cozy den. But at the height of summer, the little lizard retreats into its den for days or weeks at a time. As the gecko rests, it gets all the energy it needs from fat stored in its tail.

Some mammals drowse for just
a few days at a time . . .

A desert hedgehog doesn't mind the
heat, but it has trouble finding food on
the hottest days of the year. To save
energy, the tiny spiny critter curls up
in a shady spot and takes a time-out
during heat waves.

Desert hedgehog
Paraechinus aethiopicus
Adult: 5 ½ to 9 inches (14 to 23 cm) long

one-half actual size

curling up to protect itself from an enemy

Riyadh Province, Saudi Arabia

... **while others sleep for weeks and weeks.**

Yellow-bellied marmot
Marmota flaviventris
Adult: 20 to 28 inches (50 to 71 cm) long

one-sixth
actual size

eating fresh, green grass

Bighorn National Forest, Wyoming, US

At the first hint of summer, a yellow-bellied marmot heads underground for some serious shut-eye. It slumbers through the hot, dry days until the grass it eats turns lush and green.

When autumn arrives, estivating animals wake up and enjoy the crisp, cool days.

Meanwhile, another group of animals searches for shelter. They nestle into warm, snug spots for a long winter's rest called *hibernation*.

YAWN, STRETCH, SLEEP!

Shhhh.

MORE ABOUT ANIMALS THAT ESTIVATE

Convergent ladybugs are common in fields, forests, and gardens throughout North America. The little beetles usually hibernate in winter and stay active the rest of the year. But in desert areas, they need to escape from the heat of summer.

The **mourning cloak** is an unusual North American butterfly. It lives in forests and sips sugary tree sap. It hibernates through winter and estivates in summer.

Ever heard of escargot? It's a **land snail** people eat. In cool weather, the shelled creature glides through the forests of Europe. As the snail estivates through summer, its body uses fifty times less oxygen, and its heart rate slows to just two beats a minute.

Most crabs live in water, but not the **Christmas Island red crab**. It lives on two small islands in Southeast Asia. When the crab isn't estivating, it scuttles around the forest in search of fallen fruit and dead animals. In October or November, the crab migrates to the coast to mate and lay eggs in the ocean.

An **African lungfish** feeds on everything from insects and worms to amphibians and other fish. As its freshwater home dries up, it sticks its head above the surface and breathes air. When the water is completely gone, it depends on estivation to survive.

Mangrove killifish live in swamps along the east coasts of Florida, Central America, and South America. For most of the year, they hunt snails, insects, and smaller fish. But during the dry season, they stop eating and pack themselves into damp, shady places on land.

When the shy, secretive **California tiger salamander** isn't estivating, it roams the forests of Northern California in search of earthworms, snails, insects, and fish. In early winter, it migrates to a small temporary pool to mate and lay eggs.

The **pixie frog** is the largest frog in South Africa, and it devours anything that fits in its mouth. The frog lives in large puddles and water holes scattered among open grasslands. Females lay up to four thousand eggs at a time, but most tadpoles become prey for larger animals.

The **spotted turtle** lives in wetlands and woodland streams along the East Coast of North America. The little reptile isn't a picky eater. It gobbles up almost anything it can find, including plants, worms, slugs, millipedes, spiders, tadpoles, salamanders, and small fish.

Many people keep **leopard geckos** as pets, but their natural home is the dry, rocky grasslands and deserts of Central Asia. When the little lizards aren't estivating, they depend on their sharp eyes and sensitive ears to help them find food and avoid enemies.

The tiny **desert hedgehog** lives in the deserts of northern Africa and the Middle East and only estivates when it can't find spiders, scorpions, and other tasty treats. Females give birth to up to six babies. The tiny hoglets are born naked, but in just a few hours spikes begin to pop out of their skin.

The rocky slopes and mountain meadows of the central and northwestern United States are the perfect home for **yellow-bellied marmots**. The medium-size mammals live in groups with ten to twenty members. They hibernate in winter and estivate in summer.

ESTIVATION *VERSUS* HIBERNATION

You've probably heard of hibernation. It's when animals rest or sleep during the winter. Estivation (sometimes spelled "aestivation") is just like hibernation—only it happens in summer.

Some animals estivate because it's too hot for their bodies to function. Others take a break because food is in short supply.

Scientists have known about hibernation for a long, long time. But they're just beginning to learn about estivation. That means you can learn about summertime sleepers right along with the researchers who dedicate their lives to understanding our world.

How can you get started? By reading the resources to the right. Then be on the lookout for news about estivating animals in magazines like *Science World*, *Science News for Students*, and *Time For Kids*.

CONTINUE YOUR EXPLORATION

Atkins, Marcie Flinchum. *Wait, Rest, Pause: Dormancy in Nature*. Minneapolis: Millbrook/Lerner, 2020.

Bancroft, Henrietta. *Animals in Winter*. New York: HarperCollins, 1996.

Hickman, Pamela. *Animals Hibernating: How Animals Survive Extreme Conditions*. Toronto: Kids Can Press, 2005.

Meadows, Michelle. *Hibernation Station*. New York: Simon & Schuster, 2010.

Miller, Debbie S. *Survival at 120 Above*. New York: Walker, 2012.

Stewart, Melissa. *Beneath the Sun*. Atlanta, GA: Peachtree Publishers, 2014.

For a Teacher's Guide and a Readers Theater, visit www.charlesbridge.com/products/summertime-sleepers.

AUTHOR'S NOTE

Sometimes I like to scan the shelves in the natural history section of my town library and see what grabs my attention. On a hot June day in 2011, I stumbled upon a 250-page tome on hibernation. It contained a single paragraph about an animal behavior I'd never heard of—estivation. And that made me curious.

To find out more, I typed "estivat" into a database of science journals, hoping to pull up papers with any form of the word—estivate, estivation, estivating. The reference sections of those initial papers led me to more resources, and soon I had plenty of material for a book.

Because there were so many great examples from every corner of the animal kingdom, I knew early on that I'd write a list book. To make the presentation engaging and emphasize the diversity of the animals, I decided to use a compare-and-contrast structure with layered text. But I struggled with voice. At first, I tried a lively, humorous voice. But it just didn't feel right for a book about inactive animals. I needed to let the topic dictate the voice, so a soft, cozy, lyrical voice was a better fit.

Next, I had to admit that my beginning wasn't working. After a year of being stuck, I realized that my introduction was buried on page eight. After cutting the first fifty words, I added to and reorganized the animal examples. Then I sent the manuscript to my editor. With her guidance, I tightened the structure, strengthened the flow and pacing, and reworked the back matter. Finally, the text was ready for publication.

ILLUSTRATOR'S NOTE

As I started thinking about how to illustrate this book, something occurred to me: I'd need to show all of the animals in sleeping positions. But I didn't want the book to feel too sleepy or static.

When I want to solve a problem, I draw. So I got to work. I drew many sketches of the animals sleeping *and* wide-awake. Eventually I realized that it might be interesting to show the animals both ways! I decided to include my small sketches of the animals being active alongside the watercolors of the animals when they are resting.

My main illustrations reveal how and where each animal estivates. At the same time, the overlaid sketchbook pages include further visual details about each animal when it is awake. As a bonus, the sketchbook pages leave room for Melissa to share more of her research.

I have dozens of little sketchbooks filled with drawings like the ones throughout *Summertime Sleepers*. I encourage all readers to carry a small sketchbook and a pen or pencil, or even a phone or tablet with a sketching app. Sometimes drawing can be the best way to figure things out or learn more about the world around us.

Selected Sources

* *Amazing Animals of the World*, Set 1, Volumes 1–10. Danbury, CT: Grolier/Scholastic, 2008.

* *Amazing Animals of the World*, Set 2, Volumes 1–10. Danbury, CT: Grolier/Scholastic, 2005.

* *Amazing Animals of the World*, Set 3, Volumes 1–10. Danbury, CT: Grolier/Scholastic, 2006.

Animal Diversity Web
http://animaldiversity.org

Maintained by the University of Michigan's Museum of Zoology, this site is an online database and encyclopedia of animals.

BugGuide.net
http://bugguide.net

Maintained by Iowa State University, this site provides information about a variety of arthropods and helps people identify them.

Butterflies and Moths of North America
http://www.butterfliesandmoths.org

Maintained by the Butterfly and Moth Information Network, this site records butterfly and moth population distribution and provides information about these insects.

Chew, S. F., et al. "Nitrogen Metabolism and Excretion in the Swamp Eel, *Monopterus albus*, during 6 or 40 Days of Estivation in Mud." *Physiological and Biochemical Zoology*. July/August 2005, pp. 620–629.

Fishman, A. P., et al. "Estivation in *Protopterus*." *Journal of Morphology*. February 2005, pp. 237–248.

Geiser, Fritz. "Hibernation, Daily Torpor, and Estivation in Mammals and Birds: Behavioral Aspects." In *Encyclopedia of Animal Behavior*, Volume 1, edited by Michael D. Breed and Janice Moore. Waltham, MA: Academic Press, 2010.

Heinrich, Bernd. *Summer World: A Season of Bounty*. New York: Ecco Press, 2009.

_____. *Winter World: The Ingenuity of Animal Survival*. New York: Ecco Press, 2003.

Moore, Bob. "Estivation: The Survival Siesta." *Audubon Guides*. September 29, 2009. Available online at http://www.audubonguides.com/article.html?id=27.

Navas, Carlos Arturo, and José Eduardo Carvalho, editors. *Aestivation: Molecular and Physiological Aspects*. New York: Springer, 2010.

Roots, Clive. *Hibernation*. Westport, CT: Greenwood Press, 2006.

Stanislaus River Basin and Calaveras River Water Use Program. *Threatened and Endangered Species Report*. Napa, CA: California Department of Fish and Game, 1995.

* *Recommended for curious kids.*

To April Jones Prince and the members of the Concord Critique Group, for their friendship and wisdom—M. S.

To Melissa Stewart, a wonderful friend who has taught me so much—S. B.

First paperback edition 2024
Text copyright © 2021 by Melissa Stewart
Illustrations copyright © 2021 by Sarah S. Brannen

Published by Charlesbridge
9 Galen Street
Watertown, MA 02472
(617) 926-0329 • www.charlesbridge.com

Library of Congress Cataloging-in-Publication Data
Names: Stewart, Melissa, author. | Brannen, Sarah, illustrator.
Title: Summertime sleepers: animals that estivate / Melissa Stewart; illustrated by
    Sarah Brannen.
Description: Watertown, MA: Charlesbridge, [2021]
Identifiers: LCCN 2016009643| ISBN 9781580897167 (reinforced for library use) |
    ISBN 9781623544898 (paperback) | ISBN 9781607348887 (ebook)
Subjects: LCSH: Dormancy (Biology)—Juvenile literature. | Sleep behavior in animals—
    Juvenile literature. | Metabolism—Regulation—Juvenile literature. | Animal behavior—
    Juvenile literature.
Classification: LCC QH523 .S74 2021 | DDC 571.7/86—dc23 LC record available at
    https://lccn.loc.gov/20160096433

Printed in China
(hc) 10 9 8 7 6 5 4
(pb) 10 9 8 7 6 5 4 3 2 1

Illustrations done in watercolor on Arches bright white cold press paper
Display type set in Berry Merry by Creativeqube Design
Text type set in Grenadine MVB by Markanna Studios Inc. and Lifetime by Swfte International
Color separations by Colourscan Print Co Pte Ltd, Singapore
Printed by 1010 Printing International Limited in Huizhou, Guangdong, China
Production supervision by Brian G. Walker
Designed by Diane M. Earley

Convergent lady beetle
Hippodamia convergens
Adult: ¼ inch (0.6cm) long

enlarged

fly

Sandia Mountain Wilderness
Cibola National Forest, New

Pixie frog
Pyxicephalus adspersus
Adult: 4 to 8 inches (10 to 20 cm) long

ripping
its cocoon

removing
its cocoon

eating
its cocoon

Botswana

...ual size

Desert hedgehog
Paraechinus aethiopicus
Adult: 5½ to 9 inches (14 to 23 cm) long

one-h...
actu...

curling up to protect
itself from an enemy

West African lungfish
Protopterus annectens
Adult: Up to 40 inches (101 cm)

Riyadh Province, Saudi Arabia

...enth
...ctual size

swimming in shallow water